THE LONDON TO BRIGHTON HISTORIC COMMERCIAL VEHICLE RUN: 1971–1995

MALCOLM BATTEN

AMBERLEY

First published 2022

Amberley Publishing
The Hill, Stroud
Gloucestershire, GL5 4EP

www.amberley-books.com

Copyright © Malcolm Batten, 2022

The right of Malcolm Batten to be identified
as the Author of this work has been asserted in
accordance with the Copyrights, Designs and
Patents Act 1988.

ISBN 978 1 3981 0742 7 (print)
ISBN 978 1 3981 0743 4 (ebook)

British Library Cataloguing in Publication Data.
A catalogue record for this book is available from
the British Library.

Origination by Amberley Publishing.
Printed in the UK.

Introduction

The London to Brighton Run had its beginnings when the Historic Commercial Vehicle Club (as it then was) was formed in 1958 to cater for the emerging interest in preserving commercial vehicles. A first rally was organised at the works of Leyland Motors on 31 May/1 June of that year, which was attended by twenty-two historic vehicles, three of which were buses. A further event was held at the premises of AEC Ltd at Southall in September that year. Over forty vehicles attended this time, including sixteen buses or coaches. Five of these were from London Transport's own preserved collection for they (and their predecessors London General) were one of the few operators to have the foresight to retain some examples of their fleet for posterity. Those vehicles present there were B 43, K 424, NS 1995, STL 469 and Q 55, all of which remain as part of their collection today. At that time they were not on public display as there was no museum to display them. They were to become exhibits at the Museum of British Transport when that opened in stages at Clapham in 1961–3. Now they are displayed either at the London Transport Museum in Covent Garden or at the Museum Store in Acton. Other vehicles were privately owned, reflecting this as yet new but growing interest. Private preservation of buses had only begun two years earlier in 1956 when six enthusiasts purchased former London General 1929 AEC Regal T 31 (UU 6646). This vehicle is also still very much alive and working, now being in the care of the London Bus Preservation Group at Weybridge.

The HCVC held a few other rallies over the next three or four years, such as at Beaulieu in 1961. Private preservation was also growing in both momentum and credibility. Two other societies, the Vintage Passenger Vehicle Society and the London Vintage Taxi Club, merged with the HCVC in 1962 to bring it to the forefront as the main voice of the movement. Some preservationists were banding together to form local societies and arrange collective covered accommodation for their vehicles. From such groupings major collections such as the London Bus Preservation Trust (founded in 1966) and the Lincolnshire Vintage Vehicle Society (founded 1959) were formed.

The HCVC organised the first London to Brighton Run in May of 1962, which attracted just over fifty vehicles. Brighton was already established as a venue for such events. There was the Veteran Car Club's run in November to commemorate the repeal of the Red Flag Act (an event which still continues to take place). There was also the British Coach Rally, which had been held there in most years since its inception in 1956 and would continue for many more years. The inaugural run was judged to be a success, such that it was back the next year and every year since then until the Covid-19 pandemic restrictions prevented this happening in 2020 and 2021.

The support of the local council has been an important consideration, with the mayor of what is now the city of Brighton & Hove on hand to present the trophies. Brighton rightly sees the HCVS run as a significant event in the city's annual calendar.

Although billed as the London to Brighton Run, the 'London' starting point has seen a number of changes. Until 1988 the starting point for the Run was usually Battersea Park, with entrants departing at intervals from around 6.30 a.m. onwards depending on their speed – some of the slowest vehicles may actually have set off from London during the previous night. The aim is to arrive at Brighton before 1.00 p.m. for the judging to commence, with prize-giving from 4.00 p.m.

From 1989 to 1995 the departure point was switched to Crystal Palace Park. This has been the main departure point in most subsequent years.

The route was mainly down the A23, with an optional stopover at Crawley. On arrival at the seafront, vehicles park up on the seafront at Madeira Drive, which is closed off to other traffic while the event takes place.

The original 1962 Run was sponsored by National Benzole, who then sponsored each year until 1973. The runs were then funded by the HCVC. However, new sponsorship arrived in 1978 in the shape of Foden Ltd, the truck builders, whose own history dated back to 1856. They were of course well known for their steam wagons in which they specialised in later years of steam production. The company had preserved a number of their own vehicles, both steam and diesel, including their first diesel lorry of 1931, and some of these took part in the Run. Foden's sponsorship continued until 1981, as did the participation of their vehicles in the Run. After the company later sold out to American owners, the preserved vehicles were passed to the Science Museum reserve collection at Wroughton in 1982 and have no longer featured.

From 1982 to 1990 the Wincanton Group took over as sponsors. The company started in 1925 as Wincanton Transport & Engineering Ltd, a subsidiary of the West Surrey Central Dairy Company. By the 1930s they were involved in bulk milk haulage and a garage business – both roles they subsequently developed and diversified from. Vehicles preserved by the group's subsidiary companies featured at Brighton during this time.

From 1991 to 1995 the event had a new sponsor in the shape of Scania, the major Swedish vehicle manufacturer, celebrating their centenary. This was a particularly exciting time as it led to a number of very interesting vehicles being brought over from Sweden each year to provide a fascinating contrast to the home-produced exhibits. Some were from their own museum collection at Sodertalje near Stockholm. They were not just Scania built either; there were vehicles from Volvo and from a now demised company called Tidaholm. Scania were also involved elsewhere in sponsoring British preservation through the Scania Transport Trust Awards and their support for the Birmingham & Midlands Museum of Transport at Wythall. But all good things come to an end and since 1996 the Brighton Run has functioned without sponsorship.

The Brighton Run features around 200 vehicles each year. These are divided into classes. In the 1971–95 period vans and lorries were split according to load capacity. Then there were classes for fire engines with open and enclosed cabs, passenger vehicles with under twenty seats, single- and double-deckers with over twenty seats, military vehicles, specialised vehicles, purpose-built taxis, and steam vehicles. On successful completion of the Run each vehicle receives a commemorative plaque. A panel of judges then inspect the entrants and there is a wide range of trophies to be awarded. With such standards of restoration on display, the judge's task must at times be quite a difficult one! Some of the awards on offer recognise the varying level of resources that may be available to would-be restorers. For instance, there is the Charles W. Banfield Challenge Cup for 'the best restoration during the past year by a Society member of limited means'.

A particular feature of the Run is that there is a rolling minimum age requirement for vehicles entering the Run of twenty-one years, which means that some of the entrants from the mid-1980s onwards would not even have been built when the Run first began! By contrast, unfortunately some of the vehicles that appeared on the earlier runs have since been sold out of preservation or have gone for scrap.

A small number of steam-powered vehicles feature each year. Inevitably Foden and Sentinel steam wagons tend to dominate this section, not least because they are the most capable of travelling the distance in a realistic time.

The Run is open to all commercial vehicles of suitable age, whether or not they are normally road going. For instance, in 1985 the Transport Trust entered a 1937 aircraft refuelling bowser.

A pair of Lacre street sweepers were regular entrants in the 1980s. Electric vehicles, e.g. milk floats, have also successfully completed the trip on various occasions.

The runs have also been a showpiece for a number of significant vehicles representing milestones in restoration achievement. The superb bus restorations by Mike Sutcliffe are always awaited with great anticipation. In 1987 he produced XU 7498, the 1924 Leyland LB5 new to London 'pirate' operator Chocolate Express. In 1989/90 it was BD 209, the 1921 Leyland G7 'Charabus' that had been exhibited at the 1921 Commercial Motor Show when new.

An important feature that helps set the Brighton Run apart from some of the other vehicle rallies and runs is the number of overseas entrants it attracts. As well as those vehicles brought over from Sweden under Scania's sponsorship, a wide range of entrants have come from mainland European countries and even from America over the years, bringing marques unfamiliar to British eyes. Of these, one of the oldest must have been the 1904 Knox fifteen-seat bus, which was brought over from the USA and completed the 1986 Run.

The continued success of the Brighton Run has been significantly due to the personalities who have helped to create and sustain it. Lord Montagu of Beaulieu was a founder of the HCVC and later its president. He regularly appeared with the National Motor Museum's 1922 Maxwell charabanc CJ 5052. Another preservation pioneer, Michael J. Banfield, was chairman and the Run organiser from 1986 until 2011. And of course, the preservationists who strived to get their latest project completed in time to meet the first Sunday in May deadline. Vehicles have sometimes participated with the paintwork hardly dry!

The Brighton Run programme is a distinctive feature that continues to provide good value. It gives detailed listings of all the vehicles entered and photographs from past events. It used to also contain feature articles on preservation, vehicle manufacturers, museum collections, etc.

With over 200 vehicles entered each year, only a small selection can be shown here, so I have endeavoured to pick some of the highlights and a number of vehicles that I have not seen again elsewhere among the selections from each year.

My policy has been to arrive at Brighton early and photograph vehicles as they arrive. I will then take further photos when the vehicles are parked up or departing. I have sometimes visited the London departure site (Battersea Park, later Crystal Palace Park) the previous evening, but I have not taken pictures along the route. Readers interested in seeing the route taken are recommended to see David Christie's book *The London to Brighton Commercial Vehicles Run 1968 to 1987*, also published by Amberley, which features the whole route in selected years.

A second book will cover the years from 1996, when the event reverted to being unsponsored to the sixtieth anniversary rally. This should now occur in 2023, as the 2020 and 2021 Runs were cancelled owing to the coronavirus pandemic.

Flashback: Vehicles That Attended the First Run in 1962

Although I did not attend my first Brighton Run until 1971, some of the vehicles that attended the original Run in 1962 have been back since on various occasions. For the fiftieth Run in 2011, fourteen of the vehicles on the original Run were entered again and were noted in the programme. A selection of these are seen below. The full list of the fourteen (in age order) is CR 1500 1912 Belsize fire appliance; DU 179 1914 Dennis Fire appliance; ED 810 1914 Dennis fire appliance; LP 8389 Dennis fire appliance; CE 6065 1919 Leyland box van; XC 8059 1921 AEC bus; NT 8738 1926 Willys-Overland lorry; UF 4813 1929 Leyland bus; KR 1765 1930 Morris van; GK 5486 1931 AEC coach; NG 1109 1931 REO coach; BXK 124 1935 Austin taxi; BXP 713 1935 Austin taxi; and AVP 366 1939 Albion lorry. Some may have not been fully restored or may have been in a different livery when they were first entered fifty years earlier.

CR 1500 was built for Southampton Fire Brigade in 1912 by John Morris & Sons of Manchester on a six-cylinder Belsize chassis and remained in service until 1926. It was sold to Billings of Guildford, who fitted it with pneumatic tyres and used it until the 1950s. It was rescued in 1961 and is one of only two known surviving Belsize fire engines. It is owned by the Enfield & District Veteran Vehicle Society.

London General K424 (XC 8059) is a 1921 AEC K type bus. The type was first introduced in 1919 as the successors to the B type and were the first to have the driving position alongside the engine rather than behind, thus making better use of the available space. Withdrawn in 1932, this was put aside for preservation by London General and passed to London Transport. After participation in the 1962 Run, this became an exhibit at the Museum of British Transport at Clapham from 1963 to 1973 and now forms part of the London Transport Museum collection.

REO NG 1109 (NG 1109) was made in the USA and imported to the UK in kit form for assembly by REO Motors (Britain) Ltd in Hammersmith. Fitted with a body by Taylor of Norwich, it worked for Reynolds Coaches of Overstrand, Norfolk, until 1954, when it was laid up and used as a chicken coop until rescued for preservation. It has 'done' the Brighton Run on many occasions, as well as here in 2011.

1930 Morris light van KR 1765 was new to a confectioners in Swanscombe, Kent, and later used by a garage in Gravesend. This was first purchased for preservation in 1959. It is now with the Southdown Omnibus Trust and kept at Amberley Museum. It now carries Southdown livery, representing similar vehicles that once served the company as service vans.

1971 – National Benzole Sponsorship

In the first few years I mainly only photographed the buses and coaches entered, so these will predominate. However, as many vehicles participate on multiple occasions, some of the vans, lorries and fire engines that were entered in these years will be seen later on.

Carrying a modern registration number and fictitious Halifax Corporation livery at the time, MJX 222J was a 1931 Leyland-bodied Leyland TD1. Formerly Jersey Motor Traction No. 24 (J 1199), this has since been given a more sympathetic 'period' UK registration as SV 6107 and has regained Jersey livery.

A more modern Leyland was former Southdown 1179 (DUF 179), a 1937 Tiger TS7 with Harrington C32R bodywork. This was one of the first vehicles to be bought for preservation in 1957. The owner in 1971 hailed from Blackpool, hence the 'Blackpool to Brighton' board on the radiator. DUF 179 now forms part of the large heritage fleet of Ensignbus, Purfleet.

Not so pristine at the time was GAM 215. This is former Wilts & Dorset 296, a 1950 Bristol L6B with bodywork by Portsmouth Aviation from the collection of Mr Hoare at Chepstow. Similar GAM 216 also survives in preservation.

Making a contrast with the British buses was this 1933 Renault TN6A series, one of the typical Paris open-back buses with STCRP bodywork and thirty-three seats. This was formerly RATP No. 2481.

DR 4902, a 1929 Leyland Titan TD1, new to the National Omnibus & Transport Co. (later Southern National), appeared at Brighton in 1972 as a tender vehicle for the HCVC. This bus was an exhibit at the erstwhile Museum of British Transport at Clapham in the 1960s and is now part of the Science Museum reserve collection kept at Wroughton.

Southdown 813 (UF 4813), a 1929 Leyland TDI with Brush open-top bodywork, was another of the vehicles that participated in the inaugural 1962 Run. This was retained by Southdown and passed with the company to the Stagecoach Group with whom it has been retained as part of their heritage collection.

JF 2378 a 1932 AEC Regal with Burlingham rear-entrance bodywork from Provincial of Leicester. This was nicely presented with a period advertising board.

Former London Transport Green Line T448, a 1936 AEC Regal with Weymann bodywork, was entered by the London Bus Preservation Trust. The trust has been a regular supporter of the Run, entering one or more vehicles each year. In 1972 they also entered G351 (HGC 130), their wartime Guy Arab II.

Perhaps the most iconic and certainly the most numerous coach was the Duple OB. First introduced in 1939, the war halted its production, but from 1945 until replaced by the SB in 1950 a total of 12,693 were built, with some 7,200 for the home market. Most, as here, had Duple bodywork. Examples are often seen at Brighton and other rallies, but this one, new in 1949 to Tait, Morpeth, I have not seen since this appearance in 1972.

Ex-Burton on Trent FA 9750, a 1950 Guy Arab III with Davies H30/26R bodywork. Unfortunately, this bus is no longer in preservation having apparently been scrapped by 1999.

Steam wagons have been a feature at Brighton most years, and in 1972 we see 1931 Sentinel DG4P type KF 6482. Sentinel were one of the main makers of steam wagons, their models featuring vertical boilers and underfloor-mounted engines. In the 1940s they switched to diesel lorries and buses, but again featuring underfloor-mounted engines.

One of the strangest vehicles to have been entered at Brighton! Thames Ironworks were shipbuilders, best known for the preserved HMS *Warrior*, but from 1911 to 1913 they began producing a passenger vehicle. Resembling a horseless carriage, this had solid front wheels of 3 feet diameter and rear wheels of 4 feet 4 inch diameter. Power was provided by a 40-hp six-cylinder petrol engine. XM 215 was new to Universal, London, and has bodywork built by Thrupp & Maberley. Eight passengers were carried inside and another sixteen precariously seated on top. This unique machine was at the National Motor Museum, Beaulieu, but is now preserved at a museum in Holland.

Seen in 1973 was former Liverpool A36 (NKD 536), a 1953 AEC Regent III with a Crossley body featuring an early style of concealed radiator. As this was further up Madeira Drive from the display area it was presumably attending as a tender vehicle for another entrant. A former Crosville Bristol L type, LFM 731 is behind in a similar capacity. Disappointing weather so I didn't take many pictures.

Entry No. 202 was another Leyland from the local Southdown company, but this time from an earlier generation. CD 7045 is a 1922 Leyland N with a 1928 Short Bros body with open top and open rear staircase. Like UF 4813 seen in 1972, it had been preserved by the company and these days is part of the Stagecoach Group heritage fleet.

Another Leyland, but this is not quite what it seems. JUB 29 is a very early Leyland TD1 of 1928 but this was rebodied in 1951 with a 1932 Eastern Counties body. Keighley-West Yorkshire K451 was originally Glasgow 72 and first registered GE 2407. It had passed to Wallace Arnold in 1944, who had re-registered it. The vehicles just visible to left and right are also Leylands.

A later Leyland. BTF 25 is a 1937 TD4c from Lytham St Annes fitted with an unusually specified Leyland full-fronted body. Note the 'Gearless bus' lettering on the radiator. This was because it was fitted with the Lysholm-Smith torque converter semi-automatic transmission system.

Not a Leyland, but a Guy. HWO 334 is a 1949 Guy Arab III with Duple L27/26RD bodywork. This was new to Red & White as their L1149 but was liveried here for subsequent owners Provincial (Gosport & Fareham). This bus is now with BaMMOT at the Whythall Bus Museum and back in Red & White colours. Alongside is ex-Gelligaer 19 (MTG 84), a 1953 AEC Regal III with Longwell Green bodywork.

Another Guy Arab and this time in colour. BG 8557 is a 1944 Arab II. Originally it would have carried a wartime-built utility body but it was rebodied in 1953 by Massey Bros. As it was parked away from the rally area it was probably not an entrant but just visiting. A Bedford OB with Duple body can be seen behind.

Also parked up on Madeira Drive was this 1951 Bedford SB with rare Thurgood body from the fleet of Moodys, Northfleet. This was withdrawn and sold into preservation in 1976, but later exported to Holland in the early 1980s.

A feature of the Brighton Runs in the mid-1970s was the number of visiting preserved vehicles that were not official entrants. These tended to park up in back streets, particularly around by the Southdown (ex-Brighton Hove & District) Whitehawk garage. Seen in 1974 was former Barton 467 (JNN 384), a 1947 Leyland PD1 with Duple lowbridge front-entrance body to Barton specification.

The Brighton Run is not just about buses, and here are a pair of lorries entered in 1974. On the left is KL 4287, a 1925 Thornycroft A1 van, and on the right GU 9205, a 1928 Dennis G van.

Two more of the 1974 lorries. VH 7926 is a 1935 Bedford WS pick-up. BXD 123 is a 1935 Dennis tanker built for Shell Mex & BP Ltd with a cab built by the operators and a 700-gallon Thompson tank. In use until 1952, it was preserved by the company and restored in 1972.

One of the famous Bournemouth double-deckers with dual entrance/exit and two staircases – a feature that was also specified on their trolleybuses. This is a 1950 Leyland PD2/3 with Weymann bodywork. Four of this batch are in preservation.

This was another year when a variety of interesting vehicles could be found parked around the back streets, and at least four are visible in this view. Nearest is HDL 280, an ex-Southern Vectis 1951 Bristol LL5G with ECW body. Behind is a former Maidstone & District all-Leyland PD2.

The buses seen in the background of the previous photograph. Leading is KCF 711, a 1957 Guy Arab IV with Roe bodywork new to Chambers of Bures, Suffolk. This is a vehicle I have never seen since, although it is still listed as preserved. Behind it is PTW 110, the 1951 Bristol L6B/ECW ex-Eastern National 4107.

Down another street was parked CFH 604, a 1939 Bristol L with BBW bodywork, ex-Bristol 1254. This later returned to active service when it became a living van with Carters Steam Fair. Behind it is that Barton PD1, back for another visit.

GW 713 is a 1931-built Gilford 168oT with Weymann C3oD bodywork, which was new to Valiant Direct Coaches, Ealing. The model was produced between 1929 and 1934 and features Gruss air springs at the front, mounted either side of the radiator. Originally saved by Prince Marshall, the Gilford is now owned by The Science Museum.

A classic 1930s Leyland VD 3433 is a 1934 Lion LT5A rebodied in 1945 with an Alexander thirty-four-seat body, formerly Alexander P721. This was owned and entered by Jasper Pettie from Fife in Scotland and driven all the way from there and back – over 1,000 miles. Alongside is London Transport STL2692, a 1946 AEC Regent II with Weymann bodywork. This survived into preservation having seen further service with Grimsby-Cleethorpes Transport.

Approaching Old Steine and the seafront at the end of its journey to Brighton, LOD 495 is a 1950 Albion Victor FT39N with Duple C31F body new to Way, Crediton. This vehicle has remained in active preservation in Devon with Hazell, Northlew.

D 1959 is a 1905 Milnes-Daimler new to Brighton Hove & Preston United. After restoration of the chassis, a replica body was constructed in 1976 and the bus was entered on the Brighton Run. This was then exported to America but has since moved on to Holland where it now resides in the Louwman Museum at den Haag, the same location as the Thames Ironworks vehicle we saw earlier.

In 1966 recently withdrawn Eastern National 2255 (ONO 59), a 1949 Bristol K5G, was bought for £145 by seven lads from Leigh-on-Sea, Essex, and converted as a mobile home. On 27 January 1967 they set off to Europe to see how far they could go. Eventually this would lead to them becoming the first people to drive a bus right round the world, with the 'Essex Bus Boys' returning to Dover on 27 August 1969. It then became a tender vehicle for the Lincolnshire Vintage Vehicle Society in which role it attended the 1976 Run. Later it was used by the LVVS as a static bookstore. Restoration started in 2015 and in 2018 it was finally fully restored to its Eastern National condition.

At the end of the rally, onlookers watch as 1929 Foden steam wagon RO 6330 is prepared for winching onto a low-loader trailer for its journey home. Foden's were the other main maker of steam wagons beside Sentinel, but unlike Sentinel they specialised in the 'overtype' design with an in-line traction engine-style boiler and engine mounted above. Final drive to the axle was by chain. This was converted to a tar spraying unit, in which form it lasted until the mid-1950s.

Making its first Brighton appearance in 1977 was T31, a 1929 AEC Regal with LGOC body. This is a particularly significant vehicle as it was the last ex-LGOC bus to work for London Transport and the first London bus to be privately preserved. Bought in 1956 for £45, by now this was owned by Norman Anscombe and had been rebuilt from front entrance to its original rear entrance style since 1974. It was also refitted from diesel to petrol engine. Today this forms part of the London Bus Preservation Trust collection.

Also making its first Brighton appearance in 1977 was ex-Leeds 139, a 1934 AEC Regent with locally built Roe bodywork. Withdrawn in 1954, it had then remained in the fleet as a mobile office and training vehicle.

Another new entrant was former Birmingham 1685 (HOV 685), a 1948 Leyland PD2/1 with Brush bodywork to Birmingham's design. This style of body was also fitted to Crossley, Daimler and Guy chassis for Birmingham around this period. 1685 had been withdrawn in 1968 and rebuilt in time for its Brighton appearance.

Interestingly this bus was not listed in the programme, so may have been a substitute for another entrant. CAP 211 was a 1940 Bristol K5G with ECW bodywork, converted to open-top seaside work by its owners Brighton Hove & District. It later passed to Thames Valley for an inland open-top service through the Thameside countryside. It has since been exported to Europe. The vehicle on the right, 800 WJH, is a Lacre Model L road sweeper, which served in Motherwell, Scotland, from 1920 to 1952.

Representing the single-deck vehicles, and another newcomer, NKO 953 is a 1950 Albion Victor FT39AN with Duple thirty-two-seat bodywork, which spent all its life until 1963 with Fuggles of Benenden, Kent.

One bus that was making a repeat visit was TF 818, a 1930 Roe-bodied Leyland Lion LT1 new to Lancashire United, later passing to Jersey in 1946. Withdrawn in 1958, it then passed to the Lincolnshire Vintage Vehicle Society in 1959. The LVVS was founded in 1959 and have been regular supporters of the Run. TF 818 was first entered in 1967.

Once again, there were several preserved buses at Brighton that were visiting but not entrants to the Run. Seen leaving Madeira Drive after the event, and about to turn onto the ramp that leads up to the high-level road, is another visitor. JVH 373 is a 1955 AEC Regent III with East Lancs bodywork from the Huddersfield fleet, where it was No. 243.

Making a first visit to Brighton, DVG 395, a 1949 AEC Monarch Mk III, spent its working life with a Norfolk brewery.

1978 was the first year that the Brighton Run was sponsored by Foden Ltd, and here we see not an entrant but a former London Transport RT promoting the sponsors. RT3200 was built in 1950 and so would have readily qualified as an entrant. Mind you, in 1978 London Transport were still running RTs in everyday service, and the last of these would not be withdrawn until 1979.

Another London Bus, CR14 is a Leyland Cub REC with LPTB bodywork. The CR class was the first in the fleet to feature a rear-mounted engine. Forty-nine were built in 1939/40 and they lasted until 1953. Two of the class have survived. The other bus, JC 5313, is a 1938 Guy Wolf with Waveney bodywork also seating twenty, and worked for Llandudno Corporation.

Another of the many early Southdown buses that have survived. CD 5125 made its Run debut in 1977 and was back for 1978. A 1920 Leyland N, it was originally fitted with a charabanc body but was rebodied in 1928 by Short Bros. Sold in 1935, it was later built into a house, complete with tiled roof. It was rescued and restored over a ten-year period. This retains the forward-control layout of early buses but has the luxury of a windscreen and pneumatic tyres.

We saw a Paris bus earlier in 1971 (see p. 9). Here is another slightly more modern version, a 1937 Renault TN4H but again featuring the open back platform and centre rear entrance that was the iconic styling of 1930s Paris. On being imported to Britain, it had been given the registration GGG 773N.

A pair of AEC Regent V buses with Metro-Cammell bodywork. VKB 900 was Liverpool No. A267, built in 1957, while LJX 215 was Halifax No. 215 and dates from 1960.

Foden may have been the sponsors but this is from their main rivals Sentinel. BRF 200 is a 1933-built S6 model (shaft drive, six wheels) with a tipper body. By the 1930s Foden also introduced an undertype steam wagon, but with road tax discriminating against steam vehicles, and the more economical diesel engine replacing petrol, they would soon after give up making steam vehicles in favour of the internal combustion engine.

PO 3922 is a 1931 AEC Mammoth lorry. In 1940 Coventry Corporation converted it for bus recovery, which it did until retired in 1974, after which it passed into preservation.

This is a 1922 De Dion Bouton street sweeper that originally worked in Menten, France, before being imported to the UK for preservation.

1979 – Foden Sponsorship

1979 was the second year that the Run was sponsored by Foden, and the first year in which I started to regularly photograph the other commercial vehicles entered, as well as the buses and coaches.

Pride of place has to go to LG 7186. This was the first diesel lorry built by Foden in 1931 and was sold to Samuel Jackson of Crewe. In later years it was burnt out but in 1956 was bought back by Foden and fully restored for the firm's centenary. When Foden were taken over by Paccar in 1980 their heritage collection including LG 7186 was passed to the Science Museum and although no longer being rallied, LG 7186 has been an exhibit in the Science Museum, London.

When Foden entered the diesel truck market, they were up against opposition from several well-established other makers. Leyland motors had started out as the Lancashire Steam Motor Company but had first produced an internal combustion vehicle range from 1905. CGC 223 was a 1934 Beaver flat truck fitted with a detachable container. First used by Hovis for carrying flour, it saw further use with a showman.

ARV 143 is a 1937 AEC Matador Mk II box van. Like the Leyland above, this finished its working life with a showman, in which capacity it served until 1964.

Also from AEC, a classic eight-wheeler. LLT 26 is a 1950 Mammoth Major that worked all its life with Tate & Lyle, sugar refiners at Silvertown. These were the sort of vehicles I would have seen every day in my younger years, living in east London.

JM 4104 is a 1938 Leyland Lynx model fitted with 29.5-hp six-cylinder engine and was making its Brighton debut.

The mechanical horse made its debut in the 1930s, starting to displace the four-legged version on local deliveries. Scammell were the principal producer and DHT 717 dates from 1938. The railway companies were major users and, as seen, this one worked for the Great Western Railway.

From Guy Motors comes NVT 979, a 1949 Guy Otter tipper fitted with a Meadows petrol engine. This was another debut entry.

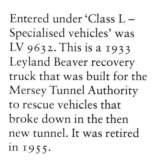

Entered under 'Class L – Specialised vehicles' was LV 9632. This is a 1933 Leyland Beaver recovery truck that was built for the Mersey Tunnel Authority to rescue vehicles that broke down in the then new tunnel. It was retired in 1955.

Not actually an entrant but on show and selling programmes, GXN 227 is a 1942 Austin K4 with a Merryweather 60 feet turntable ladder built for the NFS in wartime. Similar GXN 205 was an entrant in 1979 while GXN 227 would be an entrant in 1980.

Representing the buses present, and making its debut, was DOD 518, a 1939 Bristol L5G ex-Western National No. 333. This has the pre-war style of high-mounted radiator but was rebodied in 1950 by Beadle of Dartford. Withdrawn in 1960, it had later served as a drivers' tearoom.

It wouldn't be Brighton without a Southdown bus or two, and this was another old-timer making its first appearance. UF 6473 is a 1930 Leyland TD1 that was sold in 1938 and went to Greenock in Scotland. It became an office-cum-store within a building, protected from the elements, until purchased for preservation in 1972. Restoration was still on-going when seen at Brighton.

A colour shot of Oldham 246 (DBU 246), a 1947 Leyland PD1/3 with Roe bodywork. The window in the stairwell is a typical Roe feature. This is part of the collection of the Museum of Transport, Manchester.

Foden made bus and coach chassis, although they were never major producers of either. In 1980 we saw MTU 296, a 1948 PVFE6 model from the local company Coppenhall of Sandbach, Cheshire, where Fodens were made. The bodywork is by Metalcraft.

Edwin R. Foden split from the family company in 1933 because he thought the future was in diesel trucks. He set up his own company ERF, also in Sandbach. Shortly after, Foden also went over fully to diesel production but the two companies remained separate entities. YD 9325 is a 1934 ERF model C15, which saw service in the West Country and remained in use until 1970.

A later ERF is DMW 582 of 1946 fitted with a dray body for brewers Ushers. This was bought for preservation in 1977.

A regular feature at Brighton, including the first Run in 1962, has been the Maxwell 1922 fourteen-seat charabanc CJ 5052, owned by the National Motor Museum, Beaulieu, Hants. Lord Montagu of Beaulieu was a founder of the HCVC and later its president.

Trojan vans were built at the same Kingston factory where Leyland lorries were refitted after First World War service. This Trojan was bodied as a bus by Strachans and dates from 1955. It was used by Napier Aircraft Co.

Making its debut Brighton Run in 1980 was former East Kent Leyland Tiger TS8 JG 9938. Fitted with a Park Royal C32R body, this was withdrawn from passenger service in 1956, but was then converted for use as a travel office, and as such remained in use right up until 1978. It was then sold for preservation in 1979.

Seen departing from Madeira Drive at the end of the day is CYD 125, a 1935 Albion platform truck with a box body.

The Brighton Run started from Battersea Park. In this year there was also a 'Wheels of Yesterday' rally held in Battersea Park on the following day, Bank Holiday Monday. Some of the vehicles that had been at Brighton stayed for this as well as there being other visiting vehicles. Thomas Fox & Sons of Blackburn sent two Foden lorries to both events. GLG 962 here dates from 1939 and was bought in 1978. Behind is AMA 105, an early example built in 1933.

1981 turned wet so I didn't take many pictures that year. Arriving at Brighton is LG 8781, a 1928 Foden steam tractor.

It would not have been very pleasant driving to Brighton in the rain in a vehicle with an open cab like these fire escapes. HY 1801 is a 1931 Leyland FT1, which was bought by Bristol Fire Brigade.

HO 6241, a 1917 Leyland 'subsidy' lorry. Following the success of a demonstration to the War Department nearly 6,000 of these three-tonners were built from 1914–1918 with 5,411 going to the Royal Air Force.

Again in 1981, there was a follow-up Wheels of Yesterday rally at Battersea Park, where the weather was somewhat better. Seen at this was CK 3825, a Leyland Lion LSC1 that had just been fitted with a new replica body. This had been preserved by Ribble, its original owners, and has now become part of the Stagecoach heritage fleet.

Taken at Battersea Park on the day before the Run is BTB 429. This is a 1936 Albion lorry that spent most of its working life with a Yorkshire cotton mill owner. It was making a first appearance on the Run.

Although this looks like a standard Leyland-bodied Leyland Titan, this 1946 PD1 model from Warrington Corporation carries a body built under licence by Alexanders. Later passing to Lytham St Annes Corporation in 1972, it passed into preservation in 1975. Also taken at Battersea Park.

Entry No. 163 was a 2-horsepower bus – literally. Entered by A. Drewitt of Epsom, this horsebus was found derelict near Dorking in 1973 and restored to original livery. I doubt if it was horse-powered all the way from London, the horses probably just working the final stage into Brighton, but it certainly made an unusual and impressive sight arriving at the seafront.

A classic fifties Foden. NGX 198 was built in 1953 for British Road Services in London and worked for them until the mid-sixties. A further ten years or so followed with a showman before preservation beckoned.

Looking very impressive with its load of roped barrels is ATE 328, a 1935 Leyland 'Hippo' six-wheeled platform truck. This had come all the way from Wishaw in Scotland to take part.

This is a 1947 Lacre street cleaning van and sweeper, registered in Bradford. Only seventeen vehicles were built to this body style and this example was found in a scrapyard in 1972. Acquired by the owner in 1977, restoration was completed for it to make a first Brighton Run in 1982.

Once again there was a rally at Battersea Park the next day and here we see a vehicle long associated with the Brighton Run. Leyland box van CE 6065 was delivered new to Chivers & Son Ltd jam makers in 1919 and worked on deliveries until 1934. It was later fitted with a water tank as a stand-by vehicle for the Chivers Private Fire Brigade in the war. It was presented to the HCVC at the first Brighton Run in 1962 and has been back to Brighton many times since.

Also taken in Battersea Park, this 1926 Sentinel Super tractor and trailer had been a Brighton entrant the previous day. Restoration was completed between 1967 and 1971. The Wheels of Yesterday Rally would switch to Crystal Palace when the departure point moved there in 1989 but declined and ceased in 1995.

The 1983 Run marked twenty-five years of the HCVS (formerly HCVC). Wincanton Group were sponsoring for the second year. They displayed NYC 943 *Apollo*, a 1952 AEC Mammoth Major Mk III, which originally served with Wincanton Transport as a milk tanker.

HPX 885 is a 1946 Bedford 'K' 30cwt truck. Used by a Hayling Island builder until 1972, it was saved and restored by United Services Garages (Portsmouth) Ltd, a member of the Wincanton group. Both this and NYC 943 above were entered throughout the Wincanton sponsorship.

Some vehicles of unusual make were entered in 1983. One of the rarer examples was this 1957 Rowe Hillmaster truck. Only about 120 vehicles were made by Rowe in Cornwall between 1955 and 1962.

We have seen street brooms made by Lacre earlier. This is a 1913-built 2-ton box van. After wartime service in France this worked for William Whiteley, provision merchants in London until the mid-1930s. Lacre was set up in 1902 as the Long Acre Motor Car Co. Ltd, shortening their name a year later. Production was at Letchworth and later at Welwyn, Herts.

In 1983 there were some entries from Sweden – a foretaste of what we could expect in future years. The Scania Museum in Sodertalje sent EUU 997, a 1927 Scania-Vabis tanker. Originally a fire engine, this was rescued from a scrapyard in 1972 and rebuilt to represent the first petrol tankers operated by BP in Sweden, on the occasion of their fiftieth anniversary. 1983 was the eightieth anniversary of Scania trucks production. The company centenary would come in 1991.

Also from Sweden was this 1937 Chevrolet lorry, originally used by the Swedish army and then by a fire brigade. The contraption on the side is a gas generator. During the war years the use of such generators for burning wood or charcoal was widespread in Sweden. As can be seen this unusual vehicle was attracting a lot of attention.

1984 introduced us to one of the superb restorations by Mike Sutcliffe. C 2367 is a 1921 Leyland G2 that ran for Todmorden Corporation from 1921 to 1927. It was found derelict in Essex, without mechanical units, where it had stood with trees growing through it for forty-seven years. Restoration took four and a half years. At the time this was the oldest restored Leyland bus.

Another Leyland, but by contrast one that had been in preservation for many years and was the veteran of many Brighton Runs. DM 6228 is a 1929 Lioness LTB1 with Burlingham body new to Brookes (White Rose), Rhyl. It later worked in Jersey until 1958 where it was registered J 2975.

Also with a Channel Islands connection, AY 785 was a 1942 Bedford new to the Army. In 1947 it went to Alderney and was modified as an airfield crash tender, remaining in use until 1977.

This 1930 Morris Commercial 1-ton ambulance was new to the Borough of Edmonton. It has been restored in the colours of the Portsmouth Voluntary Ambulance Service.

Looking very rakish is this 1939 Citroen, which had been brought over from Holland. It was one of six used by the Ville De Bourg En Bresse, France, for parks and garden maintenance.

Entered by Marks & Spencer PLC and restored to celebrate their centenary, this is a 1931 Beardmore 'Cobra' tractor unit and trailer, the only known surviving example of this model. It spent most of its working life with a London brewery. Beardmore were better known for making taxis but from 1931 they began the UK manufacture of a range of these US-designed vehicles.

Entered among the 'Specialised vehicles' class, this wartime 1943 Austin K2 was fitted out as a canteen unit and worked for the No. 2 Fire Service in London.

Another vehicle entered by the Wincanton Group was this 1934 Guy Wolf 2/3-ton truck fitted with a Meadows engine.

A Swiss-made Saurer 1926 platform truck but with right-hand drive, this was found in France in 1980 and since has been completely dismantled and renovated.

Entered by Scania in 1985, this is a 1932 Scania-Vabis forty-four-seat bus. Known as the 'Bulldog' type because of its frontal appearance, this was the first forward-control Scania PSV to be built. It saw twenty-five years' active service near Gothenburg.

Leicester City Transport 329, a 1939 three-axle AEC Renown with Northern Counties bodywork. This had been acquired by the Vintage Passenger Vehicle Society, one of the constituents of the HCVS in 1958, and had been an entrant at the rally held at the Southall AEC works in that year. The bus is on permanent loan to Leicestershire Museums, who completed the restoration and entered it in the Run.

All sorts of strange vehicles have been to Brighton and this is one of the oddest. Entered by The Transport Trust, this is a 1937 Thompson petrol bowser, which was used for refuelling aircraft. It is fitted with a Ford engine.

A superb streamlined tanker lorry. This 1963 Foden K6G with bodywork by Butterfield carried liquid glucose to chocolate factories. It was purchased for preservation in 1977 and restored in 1984.

The sun came out in the afternoon. Seen leaving the seafront at the end of the rally is this Bristol tractor unit and trailer. Bristol Commercial Vehicles had become nationalised along with its parent Bristol Omnibus in 1948. Thereafter its buses were only available to nationalised bus companies, but the company also built lorries and trailers for British Road Services, also of course state owned. This HA model dates from 1956.

The hybrid bus is nothing new. Tilling Stevens manufactured buses with petrol-electric transmission until the 1920s. DB 5070 of 1925 worked for North Western. Discovered derelict in 1971, a replica body was made by Wyatt in 1984 to complete its restoration.

Representing the steam entries, this superbly presented Foden wagon dates from 1931, although it was still on solid tyres. This was the same year that the company made their first diesel lorry (see p. 31). It was new to Derbyshire Council as a tipper and had been entered on the Run in 1972 with a tipper body. Foden No.13848 is now resident on the Isle of Man.

Not surprisingly, the model 'T' Ford can usually be seen at Brighton and the engine, chassis and cab of this 1925 example are original. The tilt-covered body was constructed from photos of a similar vehicle operated by F. W. Bullen in his removal business. This was making a first entrance in 1986. This was entered by Bullens, a member of the Wincanton Group.

We saw a Sentinel steam wagon earlier. This is a Sentinel diesel lorry, dating from 1950. Like their steam wagons, the Sentinel lorries were unusually fitted with underfloor engines. Sentinel sold out to Rolls-Royce in 1956, ending truck and bus manufacture, although Rolls-Royce kept the Shrewsbury factory for many years as a site for making diesel engines.

Some rare makes of truck could be seen in 1986. This is a 1949 Vulcan 6PF, which as the side lettering states was made by Tilling-Stevens at Maidstone. Vulcan had sold out to Tilling-Stevens in 1937, but Tilling-Stevens themselves would sell out to the Rootes Group in 1950 and production of both names ceased soon after.

Even rarer is this Proctor Mk 1 tipper, built in 1947. It is fitted with a Perkins P6 diesel engine and entered preservation in 1977, the only known survivor. Proctors were built at Norwich from 1947 to 1949 and then their agent Prail's of Hereford bought the remaining parts and continued production until the stock was exhausted in 1952, with only a few hundred being built.

This 1934 AEC Mammoth Major tanker was owned and entered by the Science Museum, who carried out the restoration. Just look at those tyres!

By contrast this Atkinson eight-wheeler dates from 1961. Atkinson were the last company to employ a traditional upright radiator, and Atkinson lorries looking very similar to this were still a common sight on the roads in the 1980s.

In the 1950s and 1960s almost all trucks in Britain were British made. However, this is a 1954 German-built MAN and this was the first of its make to be operated in the UK. It was based in Scotland where it was used to transport submarine engine spare parts to naval depots. A debut entrant.

We saw a Vulcan lorry, built by Tilling Stevens. This is a rare post-war Tilling Stevens Express coach, one of three similar vehicles supplied to Warren (Altonian Coaches) of Alton, Hampshire, in 1947. The bodywork is equally rare, being by Scottish Aviation. This vehicle was still in use as late as 1981, and I had indeed photographed it before in service at Brighton in 1971.

Not a minibus, but a proper coach-built body by Reading (Portsmouth) on a Morris Commercial van chassis to produce this neat little fourteen-seater.

From the sublime to the ridiculous? This is a 1904 Knox, built by the Knox Automobile Company, Springfield, Massachusetts. Seating fifteen, it has a two-cylinder air-cooled petrol engine, two forward and one reverse gears, and a heady top speed of 10 mph. This had been brought all the way from California to take part.

Another odd-looking contraption, this is a 1913 Renault road sweeper that once kept the streets of Paris clean. A rotating brush hangs between the enormous rear wheels.

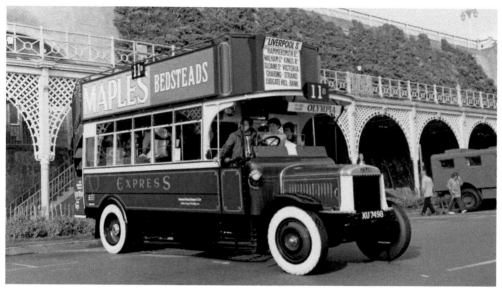

The main star of Brighton 1987 was the first rally outing of the latest magnificent restoration by Mike Sutcliffe. XU 7498 is a 1924 Leyland LB5 with bodywork by Christopher Dodson, which was new to the London 'pirate' bus operator Chocolate Express. The body was found on a farm in Norfolk in 1984 where it had been used as a store shed. An engine was also found here. Part of a chassis frame and gearbox were found in a factory attic in London, and other parts sourced elsewhere to begin the restoration. This won the Outright Concours d'Elegance award.

Because of the twenty-one years minimum age limit for entrants, by now it was possible to see vehicles with year suffix registrations being entered. Here we have a late model Bristol MW6G of 1965 with dual-purpose ECW body. This was new to Midland General in whose colours it has been restored.

An unusual lorry was this 1956 Jensen platform lorry, which had been retained by its original purchaser. The Jensen lorries were constructed from light alloys to give an unladen weight of less than 3 tons. This example was exhibited when new at the Earls Court Commercial Motor Show. By its side is a 1939 Harrods electric delivery van.

An example of an early (1928) solid tyred, chain-driven Scammell articulated lorry with a low loading machinery carrier trailer. This was new to E. W. Rudd of London.

A First World War Thornycroft J mobile anti-aircraft gun lorry, a survivor of the 182 supplied to the WD in 1916/7. This was acquired by the Imperial War Museum in 1983 and had been entered by them after restoration by Richard Peskett.

This 1933 Sentinel S4 steam wagon was entered by its preservationists in Holland. It has since been repatriated and regained its original UK registration UJ 2225.

An ambitious attempt was to enter a 1917 Fowler ploughing engine on the Run. Unfortunately NO 5 did not manage to complete the journey under its own power and arrived at Brighton on a low-loader.

Appearing at Brighton on the Run but not a programme entrant, MNA 491 was a 1937 Volvo. This was a refuse collection vehicle fitted with a Norba air-operated dustless loading system. After forty years of service in Gothenburg this had been discarded and was found in a scrapyard in 1985. It was recovered and restored by Norba and sent to England to display in an exhibition and also at Brighton.

An unusual overseas entrant in the 'specialised vehicles' class in 1988 was this 1938-built Lanz 'Bulldog' road haulage tractor. This tractor was used by the German army during the Second World War. It was entered by Jvan Veen from Holland.

One of the smallest entrants, NYE 693 is a 1953 Reliant Regent 10cwt three-wheeler van. It was new to a bakery in Lewisham but has been restored as a tyre service van, complete with authentic equipment inside.

Entered by Daimler-Benz AG, Stuttgart, West Germany, this 1932 Daimler-Benz LO2000 dropside truck had been restored by its makers to original specification.

Entered by Harrods Ltd, this is a survivor from a fleet of sixty American-built Walker electric vans and was built in 1919. Bought by Harrods in 1930 and in use until 1961, this attended the first Run in 1962.

Representing the final development of the 'Mechanical horse', this Scammell Townsman three-wheeler dated from 1966. It was new to British Rail and transferred to National Carriers in 1967.

In the 1980s the import of American fire engines began to become popular. This is a 1956 GMC, which served at Morehead City, North Carolina, all its life. It was imported to the UK in November 1987.

Burrell showman's road locomotive No. 3949 *Princess Mary* was new in 1923 to Billy Nichols of Forest Gate, London, and later sold to Charles Presland of Tilbury. Now preserved in Dorset, it completed the Run hauling a pair of showman's trailers just as it would have hauled during its working life. Once on site the showman's engines helped to erect the rides, often being fitted with a crane jib at the back, then generated electric power and light for the rides with their front-mounted dynamo.

At the end of the day, the showman's trailers are removed by Harris's AEC Matador JPX 70. This was not a rally entrant but a wartime-built lorry still in commercial service with this vintage fairground operator.

Another year with excellent weather throughout. Brought over from Switzerland, 1914 Fiat type 15 truck had been supplied new to the French Army.

Imported from France in 1980, this is a 1910 Renault. Originally built as a taxi, it was converted to a van during the First World War. Just a pity about that non-period registration it was given at the time.

Some superb signwriting on FT 6028, a 1947 Albion FT3 pantechnicon entered by and restored in the colours of G. H. Lucking & Sons of Steyning, Sussex.

It's a Leyland, but not as we know it! This 2-ton model was made at the Standard-Triumph plant in Coventry after their takeover by Leyland Motors. Some 3,000 were built with most going to South America. This one was used for internal transport at the plant. A Ferguson four-cylinder diesel engine and Rootes gearbox are fitted.

Owned by Dennis Brandt, this 1916 Foden wagon was supplied to the War Department and sent to France to assist in improving the roads behind the lines. Acquired in 1975, it was restored to original form and livery.

Mike Sutcliffe was back with the 'Charabus'. A 1921 Leyland G7, the bodywork is a cross between a charabanc and a bus. This was on show at the 1921 Commercial Vehicle Show and then worked for United Counties from 1921 to 1927, later becoming a mobile shop.

Entered by the Norwegian Science Museum in Oslo, this 1931 Ford AA originally worked for an Oslo brewery and was donated to the museum in 1970. It carries a wood gas generator with wood consumption given as 4 K kg per 10 km.

This 1933 Mercedes-Benz fire appliance was a special exhibit brought over by Daimler-Benz AG, Stuttgart, Germany.

1990 was again blessed with dry sunny weather. That would probably be appreciated by the crew of entry A1, one of the oldest vehicles to have completed the Run. This Decauville was built in 1901 and its 'detachable tonnau' design enabled it to have a choice of three bodies – two- or five-seater car or van.

The humble electric milk float – in this case a 1946 Brush. It was new to the Portsea Island Mutual Co-operative Society and following rebuilding after an accident in 1963, it remained in use until 1981.

Another Co-op vehicle. This 1945 Albion worked for the Belfast Co-op, who built its body.

Although sponsorship by Scania was not due to start until 1991, the year of their centenary, four vehicles were brought over for the 1990 Run. This 1925 Scania-Vabis twenty-four-seat bus was the first bus supplied to Swedish Railways.

This is a 1928 Scania-Vabis 3256 tipper truck. In 1936 it sank into a frozen lake where it remained until rescued some fifty years later.

Two Volvo buses were also sent over from Sweden. MFX 834 is the only surviving member of a batch of twenty-five Volvo LV72DS buses from 1935.

The other Volvo bus is a 1937 LV79D model with twenty seats. After withdrawal it had been stored in a barn from 1955 to 1985.

Restored by Barry Weatherhead, this 1925 Tilling Stevens petrol-electric bus ran in London until 1932 when it was sold to a showman. It was found built into a chalet in 1979 with no mechanical or electrical units and restored to the condition seen here.

You might not think of this as a commercial vehicle, but it is eligible! This is a 1943 GMC DUKW amphibious vehicle used for transporting troops from ship to shore. In fact, a number of these vehicles/craft were used by Duck Tours from 2000 until 2017 for sightseeing tours in London that included a trip along the River Thames.

1991 – Scania Sponsorship

The years from 1991 to 1995 were probably the most interesting because of the vehicles brought over from Sweden each year under the Scania sponsorship, so these will be prioritised in the following photographs.

Seen at Crystal Palace Park the previous day is BSW 170, a Scania-Vabis dual-door bus.

This Scania-Vabis fire engine was also entered.

Also from Sweden came this 1959 Volvo L395 Titan Turbo tipper. This model was the world's first series produced vehicle to be fitted with a turbocharger when introduced in 1954.

Two visitors from Germany seen together at Crystal Palace. SF-K-427 is a 1959 Opel Blitz fire pump that was in use by a factory until 1990. Alongside is an American-built Nash Quad with four-wheel drive and four-wheel steering.

Another view of the 1915 Nash Quad, this time at Brighton.

1991 brought another Mike Sutcliffe restoration. This 1913 Leyland was found totally derelict in the grounds of Welllingborough sewage works where it had been used as a store. It has been fully restored to the original owners' livery.

Also dating from 1913 is this Albion A12 lorry, built as a demonstrator and later sold to a Glasgow operator.

Looking more like a tinplate toy than a real vehicle is this Trojan van dating from 1934.

Only ten of the AEC Mammoth Major Mk II model from 1936 were built, and nine went to J. Lyons & Co. This one saw further service with a showman until 1968 before being sold into preservation.

Just oozing style is this 1953 Scania-Vabis B83 coach with raised observation deck at the rear.

Entered from Sweden is this 1929 Scania mobile post office. Only three were built and this was the last survivor in use until 1957. The body dated from 1940.

A Scania-Vabis flat truck dating from 1932. This worked for a sugar factory and was later converted as a fire engine.

What a splendid taxi! During the early life of this 1909 Vabis the body was fire damaged and replaced. The taxi was dismantled and stored in the 1930s and bought by the Scania museum in 1984. An original style body was eventually found after twenty years.

They don't make them like that over here! This can only be an American fire truck and consists of a 1949-built aerial ladder with a 1969 Oren tractor unit. This served with Richmond, Virginia, until imported to the UK in 1991.

A pair of ambulances now. A 1949 Daimler DC27, of which nearly five hundred were built. This was new to St Bartholomew's Hospital in London.

DDA 70 is a 1933 Guy Wolf and was the works ambulance for Guy Motors factory at Wolverhampton. Owned and entered by the Ambulance Museum at Plymouth.

A real one-off. This is the only known Caledon to survive out of the 705 vehicles built by Scottish Commercial Cars in Glasgow during their eleven-year existence. ED 1709 dates from 1919. Last taxed in 1926, it was found in use as a shanty home in the Lake District in 1971.

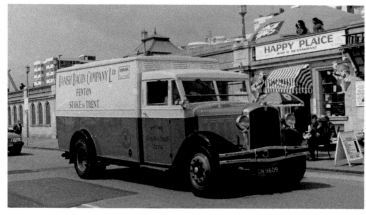

Gilford were an innovative company who started in 1926 and built bus and coach chassis with front air springs and even introduced a front-wheel-drive double-decker before their demise in 1937. This AS6 model was supplied as a box van to the Danish Bacon Co. in 1931.

Photographed at Crystal Palace YU 9464 is a 1927 Albion LK35 flat platform lorry. The design was innovative for the period with the radiator flared to the cab and the driver sitting alongside rather than behind the engine. It was the winner of three awards at Brighton.

Only eighteen of these Scammell 'Showtracs' were made, intended as replacements for the showman's steam tractors. This one was travelled until 1974, then lay derelict until purchased for preservation. It is seen arriving at Brighton with a typical showman's living van in tow.

Seen at Crystal Palace is a 1928 Volvo LV40 type sixteen-seat bus, one of the first type of Volvo buses ever built.

A Volvo LV4 four-cylinder engine truck from 1928. Five hundred were made until a six-cylinder engine superseded them.

GFS 766 is a 1933 Volvo fire pump that served at Ljungby fire station from 1933 until 1971 when it was placed into preservation.

This 1934 Dodge K34 lorry was exported to Sweden. Later converted to a fire engine and used until 1969, it was converted back into a lorry in 1971.

A 1962 Scania-Vabis LT75 lorry. The 75 series was introduced in 1958, and with improvements continued until 1980. They were available as four- or six-wheelers with a carrying capacity of from 12.6 to 22 tons.

One of the first manufacturers of motor vehicles in Sweden was Tidaholms Bruk. They produced around 1,000 motor vehicles between 1903 and 1934. This 1927 Tidaholm 45-hp lorry is an ex-fire engine restored by volunteers in the Swedish Road Haulage Association.

One of the oldest – and smallest – vehicles to have made the Brighton Run must be this 1899 De Dion tricycle. It was purchased new by the Dunlop Tyre Co. for advertising purposes but proved to be too slow. It was no stranger to Brighton having completed many veteran car and motorcycle runs. On this occasion it was appearing with a detachable goods trailer.

Imported from America for preservation is this type IC41 AFC Brill. This was the last model to be introduced by the American Foundry Company before their demise in 1952. The coach was operated by Trailways between Utah and New York.

Mack Bros of Brooklyn, New York, made their first vehicle in 1902. In 1916 they introduced the AC model or 'Bulldog' and this was the first one off the production line. Brought over from America, the vehicle was in original condition, including the paintwork. Its arrival at Brighton was celebrated by the crew with typical Yankee exuberance!

Seen at Crystal Palace, this Scania-Vabis type 840 bus dates from 1928 when it was delivered to Stockholm City Omnibus AG. This is another vehicle from the Scania collection at Sodertalje.

Also seen at Crystal Palace is this 1934 Scania-Vabis lorry from the Scania museum collection.

This 1928 Chevrolet from Sweden was built as a lorry but converted locally to a fire engine in 1934.

A 1946 Volvo type LV142DS lorry fitted with a gas producer. It was used until 1955 for goods transport and fitted with a snowplough in winter.

No stranger to Brighton! This 1935 Dennis Ace tower wagon was used by Brighton Corporation for maintaining tram, and later trolleybus wires. Sold in 1962, it passed through two owners without being restored. Found at Twickenham in 1990 in a dismantled state and restored over a two-year period.

This 1925 nineteen-seat Tidaholm bus was restored by volunteers in the Home County Association of Tidaholm in co-operation with Tidaholms Museum.

This Volvo LV61 model was used from 1930 to 1939 with two alternative bodies. On weekdays it was a platform truck to carry vegetables, but on Sundays this was swapped for this eighteen-seat coach body for outings. It was hidden in a barn soon after 1939 and later discovered and restored.

This Swedish Volvo B513 thirty-five-seat bus dates from 1948 and has bodywork built by Hoglund.

Also visiting from Sweden was this 1947 American Ford pick-up truck, which had been imported into Sweden in 1989 for preservation. American pick-ups of the 1940s and 1950s were also becoming popular with British preservationists by the 1990s and could be seen at various vehicle rallies.

Entered by the Amberley Chalk Pits Museum, Sussex, where it was restored, was this 1914 Tilling Stevens TS3 bus from Worthing Motor Services, the predecessors of Southdown. The body dates from 1909 and had been used as a garden shed in Bognor Regis from 1927 until rescued in 1971.

This 1959-built Daimler Benz lorry had started life with the German Air Force who later gave it to the Holstein brewery. It had been imported to Britain to promote and advertise German beer and lager products.

Acknowledgements & Bibliography

Most of the information about the HCVC/HCVS and the Brighton Run entrants has come from the excellent and comprehensive programmes produced for the event each year.

Further information about vehicles has come from:
PSV Circle, *Preserved Buses* (Barking, The PSV Circle, 2018)
Johnson, Brian, *The Traction Engine Register* (Horsham, Southern Counties Historic Vehicles Preservation Trust, 2016)

Also recommended:
Christie, David, *The London to Brighton Commercial Vehicles Run 1968 to 1987* (Stroud: Amberley, 2018)
Jenkinson, Keith A., *Preserved Buses* (Shepperton: Ian Allan, 1978)
Jenkinson, Keith A., *Saved for Posterity: Bus and Coach Preservation* (Stroud: Amberley, 2018)
Klapper, C. F., *British Lorries 1900–1945* (Shepperton, Ian Allan, 1973)